THE BEST
DOG MEMES
EVER

THE BEST DOG MEMES EVER

An Hachette UK Company
www.hachette.co.uk

Summersdale Publishers Ltd
Part of Octopus Publishing Group Limited
Carmelite House
50 Victoria Embankment
LONDON
EC4Y 0DZ
UK

www.summersdale.com

Printed and bound in China

ISBN: 978-1-78685-783-5

Substantial discounts on bulk quantities of Summersdale books are available to corporations, professional associations and other organizations. For details contact general enquiries: telephone: +44 (0) 1243 771107 or email: enquiries@summersdale.com.

THE BEST
DOG MEMES
EVER

When you
accidentally like
a six-week-old
photo on
Instagram

summersdale

WHEN MONDAY ROLLS AROUND AGAIN

THEM: HERE COMES YOUR CRUSH - BE COOL

ME:

EARLY MORNINGS
GOT ME LIKE:

PROFILE PICTURE

WHAT YOU THINK YOU
LOOK LIKE AT A FESTIVAL

WHAT YOU ACTUALLY LOOK LIKE

WHEN YOUR FRIENDS MAKE PLANS WITHOUT YOU

WAITING TO SEE IF YOUR DATE IS GOING TO OFFER YOU THEIR LEFTOVERS

WHEN YOU REMEMBER THAT AWKWARD THING YOU DID EIGHT YEARS AGO

WHEN YOU TURN TO THE COLD SIDE OF
THE PILLOW AND YOU'RE TRANSPORTED
TO A WHOLE NEW LEVEL OF BLISS

WHEN THE TUNES
ARE ON POINT

WHEN THE PERSON YOU
HATE BREATHES AIR

WHEN YOU SAID
THIS WAS GONNA
BE YOUR YEAR
BUT IT'S HALFWAY
THROUGH AND
YOUR LIFE IS STILL
NOT TOGETHER

WHEN YOU AND
YOUR BEST FRIEND DO
EVERYTHING TOGETHER

WHEN YOU'RE
APOLOGIZING TO BAE

WHEN SOMEONE SAYS SOMETHING STUPID AND YOU'RE TRYING TO DECIDE WHETHER TO ROAST THEM OR LET THE ISSUE LIE

MAKING PLANS WHEN
YOU'RE IN A GOOD MOOD

HEARS FOOD BEING OFFERED ROUND

ME:

PRETENDING YOU'RE IN A PHOTOSHOOT
WHEN THE LIGHTING IS GOOD

WHEN YOU TELL A JOKE AND YOUR PARENTS TURN IT INTO A LECTURE

WHEN YOU'VE ARRANGED TO MEET
YOUR FRIEND AT 6 AND IT'S 6.03

FRIENDS: YOU'RE SO EXTRA
ME: I DON'T KNOW WHAT
YOU MEAN

WHEN YOU WANT THAT SUMMER
BODY BUT YOU REALIZE YOU
GOTTA WORK FOR IT FIRST

ME WATCHING
KARMA TAKE DOWN
PEOPLE WHO'VE
BEEN BAD TO ME:

"THERE'S FOOD IN THE KITCHEN"
ME:

**STALKING YOUR CRUSH AND ENDING UP
ON THEIR SISTER'S BOYFRIEND'S AUNTIE'S
MOTHER-IN-LAW'S BEST FRIEND'S PAGE**

WHEN BAE SAYS
YOU LOOK PRETTY

ME: *HAS SECONDS OF DINNER*
THEM: AREN'T YOU SUPPOSED TO BE ON A DIET?
ME:

WHEN YOUTUBE PLAYS AN ADVERT YOU CAN'T SKIP

LEAVING WORK ON FRIDAY

GOING BACK IN ON MONDAY

**WAITING FOR THE PIZZA
DELIVERY GUY LIKE:**

WHEN YOU'RE SEVEN MONTHS DEEP INTO YOUR CRUSH'S INSTAGRAM FEED AND YOU ACCIDENTALLY CLICK "LIKE"

WHEN DOING A FAVOUR FOR A FRIEND GETS OUT OF HAND

MUM: TIDY YOUR ROOM
ME:

ME WHEN I STEP IN A WET
PATCH IN MY SOCKS:

ME AFTER SUCCESSFULLY PUTTING TOGETHER ONE PIECE OF FLAT-PACK FURNITURE:

WHEN YOU'RE TRYING TO WATCH A TV SHOW BUT ALSO TRYING TO FIGURE OUT WHERE YOU'VE SEEN THAT ACTOR BEFORE

AFTER LISTENING TO ANY SONG THAT
SOUNDS SLIGHTLY EMO AND FEELING
LIKE A WHOLE NEW PERSON

WHEN SOMEONE DOESN'T ANSWER YOUR TEXT WITHIN 0.05 SECONDS

HOW YOU
ANSWER FACETIME
WHEN BAE IS
CALLING YOU

WHEN YOUR MUM MAKES YOU TAKE YOUR YOUNGER SIBLING WITH YOU WHEN YOU GO OUT

WHEN YOU WANT TO GO TO McDONALDS
BUT MUM SAYS THERE'S FOOD AT HOME

FEELING LIKE A BONA FIDE FREE
SPIRIT AFTER ONE MUSIC FESTIVAL

**WHEN YOU CALL
SOMEONE "DUDE"**

WATCHING AN ACTION MOVIE AND BELIEVING THAT YOU ARE NOW A SUPERHERO

BECOMING MOTHER NATURE AFTER PUTTING A BUG OUTSIDE INSTEAD OF KILLING IT

WHEN YOU THOUGHT YOU GOT LEFT ON READ...

... BUT THEN THEY REPLY

MUM: DINNER WILL BE READY AT SIX

ME AT 5.59:

WHEN YOU VISIT
YOUR GRANDPARENTS

TRYING TO WAIT UNTIL IT'S ACTUALLY LUNCHTIME TO EAT YOUR LUNCH

WHEN YOUR FRIEND LIKES HUGS
BUT YOU'RE THE AWKWARD ONE

THEM: DON'T JUMP TO CONCLUSIONS

ME:

WHEN YOU'RE ANGRY BUT PEOPLE WON'T TAKE YOU SERIOUSLY

IMAGE CREDITS

If you're interested in finding out more about our books, find us on Facebook at **Summersdale Publishers** and follow us on Twitter at **@Summersdale**.

www.summersdale.com